In my humble opinion, there is no issue facing the soul of the American church more pointedly than that of abortion. How to end abortion and bring healing to the women and men who have been caught in its deception? *Loved* by Elizabeth Sharon Ann, is a jewel of the pen that addresses such an obvious, yet unspoken, need in the fray of the abortion dilemma. Can we create an atmosphere of safety and love for women to bring their participation in abortion to the light of God and receive forgiveness?

Alas, abortion is not just a woman's problem to deal with. Men who lack understanding, sympathy, courage, and the capacity to assume responsibility for their actions are equally responsible for the tragedy of abortion.

Loved by Elizabeth Sharon Ann is a desperately needed book. Thank you, Elizabeth, for the mettle to shed light on the pathway of healing for others by sharing your story.

Tim Cameron
Educator, author, and husband of fifty years

LOVED

A powerful story of redemption and restoration
for those who have lived with the pain of abortion.

ELIZABETH SHARON ANN

26 25 24 23 22 21   9 8 7 6 5 4 3 2 1

LOVED
Copyright ©2021 Elizabeth Sharon Ann

Published by:
Emerge Publishing, LLC
2109 E. 69th Street Tulsa, Oklahoma 74136
Phone: 888.407.4447 • www.emerge.pub

Library of Congress Cataloging-in-Publication Data:
ISBN: 978-1-954966-02-4   Paperback
E-book available exclusively on Kindle at www.amazon.com

BISAC:
SOC046000   **SOCIAL SCIENCE** / Abortion & Birth Control
REL012110   **RELIGION** / Christian Living / Social Issues
REL012130   **RELIGION** / Christian Living / Women's Interests

Printed in the United States of America

CONTENTS

INTRODUCTION
BY
ELIZABETH SHARON ANN

My dear friend,

Abortion recovery is a tender path. Although many of us know God forgives, living in the truth of forgiveness after abortion can be a struggle. I believe as you read the pages of my book, and work through the journal pages, you will understand freedom comes through Christ and understanding the fullness of His love for you!

My story is about the reality of what's been happening in our world, silencing the voices of babies, and silencing the voices of those who had an abortion or participated in making it possible. If you aren't one of the knowing participants, think about this idea: If you are in a room with three to four women, one of those women has likely had an abortion. It's for this reason that I share the details of my story.

To my sister who uses this book for your healing journey:

In the journaling section I ask you to pause and pray, reflect and write. Words carry more than a story. Uplifting words speak life and destructive words damage. If I say to myself "no one will ever love me because I had an abortion", those words damage our heart. On the other hand, if I say to myself "women will feel my love for them through my story," those words speak life into our heart. Please use this tool. Journaling will give you a chance to release your pain and walk into healing. This is your private moment to let go and give it all to God.

Take your time. You may find that reading a couple of chapters a week is enough. Writing will help ease the pain inside, which some of you have carried for so long, and release it. Take the first step, write the first word. Freedom takes a step of courage in the midst of discomfort. I am with you in heart as you bravely step. More importantly, the Comforter - Holy Spirit - God - Jesus - all together, hold you. You are wrapped in the arms of love. You can do this. You are safe. You are loved.

My heart holds complete love for you because I was given complete love by my Father God. You are stronger than you can imagine.

With courage, we begin....

CHAPTER 1

A Love Story

"The best use of life is love - the best expression of love is time - the best time to love is now" Rick Warren

This is a love story. My true story of God's unconditional love.

Piercing light blinded me as I slowly opened my eyes. It was disorienting and I blinked trying to make it go away. It wouldn't. Is this the present or the future? Is this real? How much time has passed? As I began to move I heard someone say, "She's coming out." I was scared and alone. Complete confusion engulfed me. There was total darkness as I slipped back into oblivion. Some of my earliest moments of awareness after my abortion seemed dream-like.

As I regained consciousness, I tried to move. I couldn't.

Feeling like cement blocks were tied to hold my hands and arms, I screamed inside, "Get out of here! Move, now!" Nothing. I could not move.

An awareness of activity around me added to my confusion. I heard a woman's voice tell me, "it's okay, you're fine, you're in recovery now and it's all over." My mind raced. "What's all over? Where am I?" As if a bomb dropped and hit me, "BOOM!" I knew where I was and why. More questions raced in my confused mind, "How did they do it? Did they cut me?" Something was wrong. I felt a trickling between my legs. It was blood. I didn't know I would bleed. "How did I not know I would bleed?" I thought to myself. "What else had I not been told?" This was my thought as I drifted back into the darkness.

Darkness grew in my mind with all the questions and confusion. It seemed to swallow me. Would I see light again? Suddenly a realization broke through the haze. I would never be the same again. What had I just done?

Everyone has "*that*" moment. Something that changes us forever. Ironically, our moments of pain allow us to understand the deeper moments of love.

As we open ourselves to recall the pain of our abortion, we begin to allow the healing power of God to pour in like warm sunlight through the window into our soul. God is not mad at you, He is not ashamed of you.

I cannot emphasize that enough. God is not mad at you! God is not ashamed of you! God loves you more than any person on this earth has ever loved you, and more than you could ever love anyone. It's true! Think of the purest love you've ever felt. God's love for you transcends it all.

As we open ourselves to recall the pain of our abortion, we begin to allow the healing power of God to pour in like warm sunlight through the window into our soul. God is not mad at you, He is not ashamed of you.

As I share my story, some of you may have had a similar experience, even down to the words used when you went to a clinic or medical office to have your abortion. Our world today has changed so much and yet in some ways it has stayed the same. We have made changes in shopping to online food orders, and even pick up and go groceries. We never have to leave our home to shop. We even have doctor's appointments online if needed. Those are changes that have definitely helped many. In spite of all our progress in our society, procedures for an abortion remain basically the same. I know this because I have regularly heard the stories. I've sat with hundreds of women through the years who have privately shared their abortion story with me, and although I haven't stepped a foot inside a clinic since my abortion, the stories are eerily similar in the procedure.

Another area of very little change, when it comes to the topic of abortion is that women and those who've helped them in their decision are hiding in plain sight. Pain is hidden behind masks of over-achievement, addiction, and worst of all...silence.

Jeremiah 16:17 "For My eyes are on all their ways; they are not hidden from My face, nor is their iniquity concealed from My eyes."

CHAPTER 1 JOURNAL

Pain transcends time. I describe the awareness of time the moment I began to come out of the thick haze of anesthesia. Some people say "time heals all wounds". The truth? Time heals nothing. Only Jesus can take your pain and heal.

"This is the message we heard from Jesus and now declare to you: God is light, and there is no darkness in him at all. So we are lying if we say we have fellowship with God but go on living in spiritual darkness; we are not practicing the truth. But if we are living in the light, as God is in the light, then we have fellowship with each other, and the blood of Jesus, his Son, cleanses us from all sin." I John 1:5-7 (NLT)

Whatever the reason you've picked up my book today, you are now more than a reader, you are my friend. Have you ever heard that another word to describe the role of the Holy Spirit is "Comforter?" I pray as you walk through my story, you will feel the Comforter wrap arms of tender loving care around you to walk out of pain and into healing from this day forward.

If you haven't written about the day of your abortion,

take some time to ask God what He wants you to see about that day.

What changes took place in your heart that day?

_____

_____

_____

_____

_____

_____

Allow Him to show you how He loved you and your baby then and now. His love for you has never changed.

_____

_____

_____

_____

_____

_____

Silence Is Not Golden

"History will have to record that the greatest tragedy of this period of social transition was not the strident clamor of the bad people, but the appalling silence of the good people." Martin Luther King Jr.

I love to talk. In fact, a gift God gave me allows me to speak to women all over the country through my ministry and my business. All the talking never included a conversation about abortion. Never. One phone call changed everything. On the other end of the phone a friend was almost inconsolable as she said, "Elizabeth you can't imagine what I've done...God can never forgive me."

"Elizabeth, I - had - an abortion." Moments felt like eternity passed until I could whisper... "So did I." It had been 20 years since my abortion. I had never told anyone.

Until I decided to have an abortion, I had never met anyone who had one, or so I thought. Events in my life led me to a girl who had an abortion a few months before mine. Ours wasn't a heart to heart conversation. We didn't cry on each other's shoulder to share why we had made this decision. After all, "my body, my choice," right? The secret to this slogan? "My choice" will affect my life forever.

"Elizabeth...I - had - an abortion." Moments felt like eternity passed until I could whisper... "So did I." It had been 20 years since my abortion. I had never told anyone.

How about you? Do you know anyone who has had an abortion? I understand there is a high likelihood that if you're reading this, you are the one. If you have felt like the only one, you're not alone. According to CDC (Centers for Disease Control) one in three women will have had an abortion by age 45 in the United States. We declare War on Drugs, War on Terror, and War on Poverty. Every day in our cities across America, there is a War on children through abortion. The old saying "Silence is golden" is a lie when it comes to abortion and the long-lasting pain it causes to everyone in the ripple effect.

Unplanned pregnancy and abortion is like throwing a rock in the water. As the rock splashes into the water, ripples begin from the center and grow across. Scientifically the object causing the ripple is called "a disturbance." Interesting. A girl finds out she's pregnant, a baby - a ripple. Plans interrupted, another ripple. The father of the baby, a ripple. Moms, Dads, Grandparents, siblings, all ripples. We fool ourselves into believing the lie that abortion is solving a problem. That "problem," a baby, is now dead, and the real problem has just been brought to life.

After my abortion I was determined to change. I would clean up my act and live the best life possible. My career in the Federal Government launched my drive to try and work away the pain. I was successful in my career. No one would ever know that with every step up the ladder of success, I was sliding down a painful slope of regret.

As I began my family, I wouldn't just be a good mom, I would be the "perfect" mom. Postpartum depression was blamed for my sadness after my firstborn. Postpartum is real. No question. However, for me, part of me felt the deepest shame. I was suffering trauma in the midst of what should have been the most glorious experience. A disconnect happens when you experience a traumatic event.

Trauma is defined by the American Psychological Association (APA) as "the emotional response someone has to an extremely negative event. The effects can be so severe that they interfere with an individual's ability to live a normal life." Sound familiar? In fact, now there is a term given to the psychological after-effects of abortion, based on PTSD. "Post Abortion Stress Syndrome." After my abortion I had no idea what a "normal life" would ever mean.

Silence was added to the darkness I felt in my soul. I had no idea if God still loved me. In fact I would go so far as to say at those moments, I didn't believe God could love me. No way.

How could I live so inconsistent with the way my parents raised me? My actions spoke louder than words. Many years have passed since I first revealed my abortion story.

So many beautiful women have sat across from me with tears flowing down their face with one question. "How did I get here?" By the time a woman is ready to ask that question she has faced multiple scenarios. Of those who had abortions, some experience similar effects to PTSD, which includes flashbacks, anniversary reactions, feeling suicidal, feeling diminished control of life and beginning or increasing drug use. Harmless? Painless? Hardly.

If you have experienced one of the mentioned traumas, you are not a statistic. You are uniquely seen by God. You are not a number or just another woman or man affected by abortion. Your life is as unique as your thumbprint. This very moment, He wants you to know He has seen every tear fall.

Psalm 56:8 "You keep track of all my sorrows. You have collected all my tears in your bottle. You have recorded each one in your book." (NLT)

CHAPTER 2 JOURNAL

I've had the privilege of speaking to so many beautiful women through the years since my abortion. When women or men find out I've had an abortion, I hear the stories never told, through a flood of tears, eyes filled with pain. I understand not all stories are the same. As you read, you may experience a flood of emotion.

Can I share something we forget sometimes? God created our emotions, all of them! Emotions are to be used for cleansing and even healing. Remember the scripture, "The joy of the Lord is your strength." (Nehemiah 8:10). Tears are made of what? Salt water - saline solution! What is used in hospitals to clean a wound? Salt water - saline solution! Our Father understood at creation we would have times of tears. He created our tears for cleansing. Let's look at the scripture again about tears. Psalm 56:8 "You keep track of all my sorrows. You have collected all my tears in your bottle. You have recorded each one in your book." (NLT)

What emotions have you begun to feel as you read?

_____

_____

_____

How would you describe your life in the first months after your abortion?

_____

_____

_____

_____

_____

What, if any, thoughts did you have about telling anyone?

_____

_____

_____

_____

_____

How long, if ever, was it until you first shared your abortion experience?

_____

_____

_____

_____

_____

How Did I Get Here?

"To get where you want to go, the first question you always have to answer is 'Where am I?' We only find out where we are when we find out where He is. We only find ourselves when we find Him." Ann Voskamp

Loving parents raised me. Hard working and determined to be the best they could, they succeeded. Certain things were never discussed. I have been on social media for years now with a Bible study and you'll hear me say "there's nothing new under the sun". Truly no topic is off limits in the Bible. However, not so with my mom. You can imagine my surprise when I was a grown woman and learned for the first time, my mom had a miscarriage after I was born. Those were topics you didn't discuss.

By the time my dad was 23 and my mom was 19, they had 4 children under the age of four, including twins. As kids, we were in church more than out. Vacation Bible School and church summer camps were normal for our family. I spent most of those at one time or another walking the aisle during the altar call. My heart was sincere and I wanted to be a "good girl." I didn't want to go to hell. I knew God loved me, and yet it seemed conditional. As long as I was a "good girl" He would love me. I can't tell you this was preached exactly, but I can tell you it was etched in my mind.

Living the simple life with my family upbringing should have been full of joy and ease. Instead, it brought insecurity and pain from an adult man who was molesting me.

Not all of life was bad. But when molestation happens, seeds are planted that grow into doubt and lies. When you are raised in an environment of secrecy, unless you go to God for freedom, it stays with you.

When dust collects on furniture, you don't really notice until there is a layer that makes it obvious - no more hiding it; in the same way, secrecy contaminates you. You don't see it happening until you are covered and it's obvious; just like the furniture, it's time to be cleaned.

Childhood trauma changes the trajectory of that child's life. When molestation occurred, for me, it lit a fire. That fire would burn inside me. I became sexually active with a boyfriend at a tender young age. I thought we were in love. For me, love was physical now. My mom found out we were intimately involved and separated me from seeing him. Our relationship ended painfully, and I resented my mother for her intrusion. Just as the roots of a tree, bitterness and resentment grow deep into our heart. Roots take hold and suck the life out of us little by little.

Roots of bitterness began growing toward my mother. I refused to let her in on any discussion of my life's dating activity. Remember that fire I mentioned? Some call it "boy crazy." Yes, that's the simplicity of it. What it was went much deeper. As I entered my late teens on my way into adulthood, I was on a quest. I wanted love, not realizing my deepest desire was the love of my Heavenly Father to heal me. I needed Him to cleanse the pain and the shame of the abuse I endured. Instead, for me, love equaled sex. My mind truly felt that was the answer. My mom was out of the conversation now and I was living in darkness and silence.

Darkness and silence once again. I was heading toward the darkest decision of my life as I spiraled out of control. It was during my first semester in college when I found out I was pregnant. My confusion of what love meant caused me to believe that when I told the father of my baby, he might tell me he loved me and would want to make everything right. He didn't. We had already broken up before I found out I was pregnant. His excuses for the breakup were lame and I felt abandoned once again. In my brokenhearted state, I called him to tell him I was pregnant. He said I wasn't his first girlfriend to get pregnant. His solution was to pay for my abortion. No words of "I'm sorry" or "I love you" from him. After he brought the money to me, I never heard from him.

Good intentions can be warped into bad decisions. My intention was to take care of the "problem" of being pregnant.

"How did I get here?" The answer was, one lie at a time.

As the "life of the party" girl, I was the one with answers, not needs. I couldn't show weakness or need. I was the problem solver. Friends came to me for answers. Pregnant, not married, and no relationship meant shame. The lies of the enemy whispered in my ear, and I would listen. Mistrust leads us to believe we can't handle difficult situations. We have to solve them, not share them.

When I asked myself,

"How did I get here?" The answer was one lie at a time. With one hidden piece of my life at a time, I stepped back into the dark. Little did I know that darkness I felt, would swallow me with my next decision.

CHAPTER 3 JOURNAL

I mentioned parts of my young life in this chapter. Included was the link for me being open to make the decision to have an abortion. I realize not everyone has what might be called a "link." However, when you pause and pray, ask the Lord to show you a part of your life before your abortion. Perhaps there was a mindset or an attitude. Not every attitude or mindset leads to abortion. I'm asking you to look deep into your soul. A seed of openness to the idea came from somewhere. Ask the Lord to show you. You might have a similar story to mine. You might have been betrayed or molested. Ask. You will receive the answer.

Were you the "good girl" or the "bad girl?"

_____

_____

_____

_____

_____

_____

_____

_____

What was your key to mistrust?

_____

_____

_____

_____

_____

What links from your past might have contributed to your decision for abortion?

_____

_____

_____

_____

_____

What is your emotional state after reading this chapter?

_____

_____

_____

_____

_____

CHAPTER 4

Nothing New Under the Sun

"What has been will be again, what has been done will be done again; there is nothing new under the sun." **Solomon**

If you grew up in the 1950's or 1960's you may remember television commercials for gum, coffee, or cereal. You can see old "throwback" commercials online. In the 70's, 80's and 90's the tone began to change. Better looking models, and advertisers discovered "sex sells." The trend grew. In the 21st Century, we have ads and TV shows with topics that we barely discussed in our families, much less in public. Not that people weren't living secret lives, just that we didn't talk about it.

The Bible is filled with stories that may shock you. At

the top of this chapter is the quote from King Solomon in Ecclesiastes. He had everything money and fame could offer. He grew to be an empty man and wrote about the monotony of life. Everything that we think is unusual and new to us, is not. Stories of adultery, child sacrifices, bestiality, and incest are all in the Bible. You'll also read some amazing stories of a talking donkey, an axe head that floated up from the bottom of water, and money in the mouth of a fish. The good news, God is creative and innovative. And He will always find a way to show you how much He loves you.

> **Society has made abortion about the woman, not the baby. The one who can't speak gets no choice, so I will choose to give my voice.**

My heart is for you to know the heart of God. You will understand His heart for you the more you take time to pray and read. I mentioned the topics and stories because at times we get blinded by current day news. We feel like things in our country or in our state or in our life are the worst ever. Yes we certainly have troubles. However ,when we understand that the same God who created the Universe created you and me, our perspective changes.

I was determined to be different from the way my mom had treated me when it came to talking about sex. I was a "good mom." My kids would be free to talk to me about anything and everything. I was completely unprepared for what that would mean.

On a leisurely drive home from a camp my sons attended overnight, I overheard their discussion in the back seat. Keep in mind these were boys around the age of 10. What was their discussion? Oral sex. I was shocked that my young boys had already been introduced to the topic of sex, even more so to have it be specific.

In today's society we feel there is freedom more than ever. Free speech, free college, free healthcare, free choice. None of the things I mentioned are free. Although our society may talk more about freedom, it seems we are bound more than ever. People fight over political views, laws, and as a whole, we continue to spout "freedom."

Society has made abortion about the woman, not the baby. The one who can't speak gets no choice, so I will choose to give my voice. My point with this is although we hear freedom of choice for abortion, our precious women still live in a shroud of secrecy.

Our political climate makes abortion a voting topic. It's merely a word now. Not a baby. Years ago I posted a video on social media showing conception through the birth of a baby. I was shocked when I was verbally attacked by a man, not a woman! He felt the need to explain to me that an "embryo" is not a baby. He went on to say that only when birth happens is it a baby. He told me that videos like the one I posted make women uncomfortable. Obviously, it struck a nerve with that man as well.

In the chance you may be a man reading my story, I'm thrilled! Thank you for having the courage to step into the world of a woman's view. A friend of mine recently told me the story of a conversation she had with a man who is a long time friend. She was telling him about my book and my story. He told her that his mom, who is in her late 70's, just shared with him a few years ago about an abortion she had before he was born. A man - a father - a son - an uncle - a brother - whatever your role, you are needed in the cycle of healing for a woman. I'm asking you to realize that if a woman opens her heart to tell you her story, hold that carefully.

A common mistake we all make, man or woman, is to think we need to fix a hurting person. We don't. We can't. Only God can.

Here are two very important things to remember when someone decides to share their story with you. First of all, let her talk. No interruptions. Second, listen with love. When they are finished, you may be tempted to offer solutions. Not a good idea. Instead maybe ask, "Is there anything I can do for you?"or "How can I help?" Or offer "I'm here." or "Can I give you a hug?" Sometimes a hug goes a long way. A hug can be comforting and empowering. Remember the old saying, "People may forget what you've said but they'll never forget how you made them feel."

When I decided to write my story, I shared my thoughts with a few of my closest loved ones. One of those was a woman who started crying almost as soon as I began talking. She had no idea I had an abortion. I made the assumption from her reaction that she must have also aborted her baby. An opening in the conversation occurred and she confessed she had paid for her daughter's abortion and her granddaughter's abortion. She was in her late 60's at the time. She had never shared with a single soul what she had done. Her comment to me was that she had lived in torment with her secret all these years.

"How am I going to tell someone not to have an abortion when I've paid for my daughter to have one?" A woman asked this question during a conversation about abortion. We are drawn into the lie that says "If I've had an abortion, I can't tell someone else not to." We don't want to be labeled a "hypocrite."

When we label sin, we create problems. We have some who believe that one sin is worse than another. The Bible does not label sin in order of worst to least. In fact, Christ died for us knowing we would sin. He had you and I on His mind when He was on the cross.

In the Bible, Romans 5:8 "But God demonstrates His own love for us in this; While we were still sinners, Christ died for us." How comforting! Whatever the reason you chose abortion, and even the fact that you chose abortion, you are forgiven! I am forgiven! Thank You, Lord!

Remember when I began this book, I told you this is a love story? Well there it is my friend: "God demonstrates His own love for us" pure love.

You are not alone. One of the biggest tools the enemy uses against us is isolation. When we believe no one understands, or even believe that we can just deal with things on our own, the lie continues. As I sat in the car driving to the abortion clinic, I felt so alone, in spite of sitting in the car with two others. How could I be so gullible?

CHAPTER 4 JOURNAL

As I began this chapter I used the quote from King Solomon in the Bible where he talks about nothing "new under the sun." Truth is, that doesn't diminish whatever pain you have experienced. What it does is remind us that as painful as life can be, we can know that we are not alone. Isolation never produces anything promising.

If you have discussed your abortion with anyone, what was their response?

_____

_____

_____

_____

_____

_____

_____

_____

_____

_____

_____

If you haven't discussed it, or your role in an abortion, what has kept you from sharing it?

_____

_____

_____

_____

_____

_____

_____

_____

_____

What do you wish someone would say to you if and when you tell?

_____

_____

_____

_____

_____

_____

_____

_____

How will you treat someone who shares their story with you?

_____

_____

_____

_____

_____

_____

_____

_____

_____

_____

What is the hardest part of sharing your story, no matter what role you have?

_____

_____

_____

_____

_____

_____

_____

_____

_____

Tornado Alley

"A teardrop on earth summons the King of Heaven." Chuck Swindoll

Most states have winter, spring, summer and fall seasons. Some have more or less of one or the other. In Oklahoma, where I live, we have an additional season. We have "tornado season". I live in "tornado alley", which simply means we have more tornadoes on a regular basis than other parts of the country.

One storm season, we had a particularly deadly, F-5 tornado hit one of our towns, killing 36 precious people. It was devastating and is on record as the highest wind speed ever measured globally. We watched the television helplessly as our local news stations broadcasted live. In the darkness of the storm you could see tail-lights. Vehicles with unaware drivers careening into a death trap! I shouted, "Turn around! No, you could lose your life! Please turn around!" Unfortunately no amount of shouting from my living room at the TV would help any of those people. Warnings from radio and television and even sirens blaring didn't stop people from danger.

We see the people standing on the corners of abortion clinics. Most of them are well intentioned. Their hearts cry out and sometimes their voices too. Some stand quietly praying while others, like a tornado siren, wail, "No! Stop! Turn around! You don't have to do this!"

No one stood on the corner of the clinic I entered. No shouts or prayers were heard as I walked up the gray cement steps. It felt like a slow-motion movie, almost an out-of-body experience.

Not that it would have mattered though. I can't say what effect a "pro-lifer" shouting or simply talking to me would have had at that moment.

Nonetheless, I was inside and like those driving into the storm didn't know a tornado was waiting to swallow everything and everyone in its path, I had no clue what disaster lay ahead for me.

The woman who prepared me for my abortion, literally told me it wasn't even a baby yet, it was simply a fetus. At my young age, I didn't have a clue what she meant by the word "fetus". It seemed cold and sterile. And I was already in a fog to some degree just being in the situation. Could I really be so gullible to believe pregnancy didn't mean a baby yet? Yes. Could it be true that giving birth is defined as a baby being born? No. Ask our modern technology to define pregnancy and here's the answer. "A woman or female animal having a child or a young, developing in the uterus." How in the world could I be so naive?

Driving from my home town with virtual strangers to the abortion clinic seemed an eternity. I was 18 and alone in my mind. My mom and I had a strained relationship. Her reaction to finding out I was having sex with my former boyfriend ended so badly I wasn't about to open myself to more ridicule. My mom would have likely embraced me in my scared state. She wouldn't have been happy that I was pregnant. But I never gave her the chance to show me what she would have done. Instead, quietly I rode inside the car with a mom and daughter I barely knew, on my way to make the worst decision of my life. How many times do we make a decision out of fear of what might happen - when most of the time, that is not the reality of what would happen. It's part of the lie to keep ourselves hidden.

Upon arriving at the clinic, we parked. I barely remember those moments. I recall the orange-red bricks of the building but not much else. I walked out of the car, alone. I lived so much of my life feeling rejected. My thoughts went immediately that they were ashamed to be seen with me.

I was not even aware this was the same clinic and the same drive that this mother - daughter pair had made a short year before. This same mother drove her daughter to get an abortion. I can only imagine what they must have been feeling.

As I walked through the door into the reception area it felt so cold inside. When my name was called I was taken to the next room. Filling out paperwork brought a dilemma. Would I use my real name? Odd as it may sound now, I wanted to be honest. So when it came to the question about birth control, I was ashamed to answer "no". Maybe I wouldn't be here if I had used birth control right? So I felt once again, the shame of getting myself into this place. My intention a few months prior to getting pregnant was to go on birth control. I went to a doctor and had my first pelvic exam. Those days, we didn't have all the privacy laws for medical information they have currently. I was petrified my mom would find out if I asked for birth control.

I sat numbly in the intake room. I was afraid. I was afraid that I was alone. No one counseled me. Would I feel pain? Would I ever be able to have children after this? Would it hurt?

As the clerk began to look over my information, she asked if I had any questions. Yes, I had questions. Simple questions. I wanted to know if this would hurt the baby. I wanted to know how big my baby was. She knew exactly how to answer me in order to put my mind at temporary ease. I don't doubt this woman believed in what she was doing. For whatever reason she may have thought she was helping me.

I am not saying by any means that men and women in the business of abortion are evil. In her book "Unplanned" by Abby Johnson, she shares the story of leaving her job as a director of an abortion clinic, to join the other side at the pro-life office. Hers is an amazing story which I highly recommend. I am for life. A story that promotes life is a story I will promote.

An "embryo." That was the word used by the woman who was answering questions about my baby.

One part of her book Abby writes about the well meaning men and women inside the abortion clinics. Some who believe they are there to help women's health, not anti-child, but pro-woman. Misguided, yes but in spite of that our call is to pray for them. We have all walked in the shoes of misguided people. Her book is a reminder to pray for those inside the clinics as well as outside.

An "embryo." That was the word used by the woman who was answering questions about my baby.

She asked if I had ever been around chickens. I grew up on a farm and we raised chickens, so "yes" was my answer. She added that at this stage, the "embryo" was no different than a chicken egg. When she asked if I had ever cracked open an egg and seen the little white glob attached to the yolk, I said "yes." Her description was to tell me that was exactly what the "embryo" looked like. There was no life, no movement and there was nothing to resemble a baby. At her estimate, I was approximately 10 weeks pregnant.

As the appointment continued my brain kept trying to convince my heart. "It was an 'embryo', all I was doing was throwing away a bad egg."

Going under anesthesia, the procedure, and recovery were all at the hands of strangers. My heart cried tears that my eyes never could.

My entire abortion experience was full of strangers. Practical strangers had driven me to the clinic. Everyone in the clinic was a stranger. Now another stranger was leading me to the room I first mentioned in this book.

Going under anesthesia, the procedure, and recovery were all at the hands of strangers. My heart cried tears that my eyes never could.

My baby girl died at the hands of a stranger and her mother. Yes, I've assigned gender to my baby. I feel strongly that my baby was a girl. I will never have proof until we're reunited in Heaven someday. Until then, she will always be held in my heart. It helped me tremendously to assign gender, it brought comfort to me.

Remember how I described the worker telling me I was probably 10 weeks pregnant and the "embryo" was basically a blob? At 10 weeks, a baby is actually a fetus.

Tissues and organs are rapidly developing. Uncontrolled movements and twitches occur as muscles. Brain and nerve pathways begin to develop. The baby's head is still bigger than the rest of her/his body at 10 weeks. His/Her brain is developing rapidly and the nervous system is responsive, with many internal organs starting to function. Gender is already established. At 10 weeks, a heartbeat is almost fully developed. Tooth buds exist, taste buds are on the tongue, a digestive tract is capable of moving food all the way to the bowels. Within a week this 10 week old baby will be able to yawn, swallow, and close eyelids. Days of thumb-sucking and head-turning are all possible within this time period. All possible with a baby as small as the size of a plumb. The beauty is that even now, at 10 weeks, true identity markings are in place making them a unique individual.

"Before I formed you in the womb I knew you. Before you were born I set you apart." Jeremiah 1:5 It would be years before I could embrace this scripture. Until that time, I would begin a spiral to grasp for any form of control and perfection I could find. I raced to find a way out of my pain from the abortion. Instead I drove into the darkness, just like those riding into the storm, unaware of the danger looming ahead.

CHAPTER 5 JOURNAL

In this chapter I shared more about the circumstances surrounding my decision for abortion. Is your memory clear of what you were told? Who was with you?

In Chapter 1 Journal I asked you to reflect on the day of your abortion. Did you identify with what the worker told me about my baby with the description of "embryo"? What terminology was given to you about your baby? If you were to assign a gender to your baby, what would you feel?

When we keep our eyes on Jesus during the process of journaling, He will show us what we need to see. Our minds are intricately made to protect us from pain. Some memories are locked away for our safety. Don't worry that you aren't remembering. When the Lord is ready for you to see, you will see and it will be for healing, not destruction. As you read questions throughout the chapters, answer whatever is comfortable. You may want to ponder the questions and come back later to write. There is no wrong or right way to do this. Remember, no condemnation, only love is extended to you here.

Courage my friend... Take some deep breaths... pray, reflect, and write.

CHAPTER 6

Hiding In Plain Sight

"It's not about finding ways to avoid God's judgment and feeling like a failure if you don't do everything perfectly. It's about fully experiencing God's love and letting it perfect you. It's not about being somebody you are not. It's about becoming who you really are." Stormie Omartian

A friend of mine, I'll call Jenny, shared about her friend from high school. For the sake of privacy we'll call her Lucy. Lucy was raised in a good home with loving parents. Her parents insisted on being in church every time the doors were open, just as so many of us experienced.

We used to call that a drug problem, my mom drug me to church on Sunday morning, she drug me to church on

Sunday night, and Wednesday night….you get the picture. Sometimes a little humor helps. Unfortunately though, so many times parents think that just having their daughter in church will make sure to prevent pregnancy. It does not. I believe that open and honest communication from parent to child about sex, about love, about what the Bible has to say on those topics, will at least open the door to understanding that God isn't against human beings having fun on earth. In fact, He created sex. And when an open conversation can happen, there can be a clearer light into why God designed sex specifically for marriage. But this is not a parenting book per say, so I will just add that many books are available in Christian bookstores and online that will help you with the conversation.

Lucy was a tender sweet girl. Her parents were good to her. Although strict, they loved their daughter as much as any earthly parent could. They would not allow her to listen to "rock music" or watch music videos on TV which had become so popular during that time. After graduating from a christian high school, Lucy began testing the boundary lines at home. She was 18 after all, and considered an adult. Her first date with a young man she had met at work ended with a night of dancing at a club. Lucy's first sexual encounter was with him in his pickup. She got pregnant. Lucy could not face her parents or anyone else for that matter. She was ashamed she had put aside everything her parents stood for and she felt she abandoned her own morals. She told the young man, now her boyfriend, about her pregnancy, and he paid for her to get an abortion.

As Lucy continued, she shared more. She told Jenny the reason she wanted to share about her abortion, was because this day, as they sat in the restaurant eating, was her baby's due date. Lucy made a statement that sent chills up Jenny's spine. She told Jenny that the night before their lunch, she had a dream and saw her baby - and it was a boy. No tears. No picket signs. No judgment. Just two friends. Heart to heart.

I had no Jenny in my life at the time that I could open up to share my pain. Instead I was hiding. Perfection became my goal after my abortion. Just one problem with that goal. It's impossible! Jesus Christ was the only perfect human on earth. Striving for perfection caused me to try and fix my problem of pregnancy with an abortion. Striving for perfection led me to try and blot out my mistake of broken relationships. I pledged all my love to a man who listened to my story. He was the first and only person to hear my abortion confession until decades later. Our marriage would be built on that foundation. He divorced his wife and married me. I became an instant stepmom to his two children.

I was hiding my heart in plain sight.

I stuffed what I had done further down with each passing day. I refused to dwell on the painful thoughts. I never talked about it again. Instead, I would fill all the void and the pain of past rejection with goals and striving for the top place in every area of life, in my career, my marriage and my motherhood.

Although I did a pretty good job of hiding on the outside, I was still seen by the God Who loved me. Psalm 34:18 "The Lord is close to the brokenhearted; He rescues those whose spirits are crushed." Even in my broken state, He loved me. I tried to walk away. God would not. He never will. I was afraid to walk into the doors of a church. How could I ever return?

CHAPTER 6 JOURNAL

Perfection can be a mask we wear to hide pain. What part of your life hides your pain? As you journal take a moment to identify your pattern. So here's what I mean... when something happens that makes you uncomfortable, maybe someone starts a conversation you don't like, or makes a comment you can't figure out how to take, or sends a text you can't be sure how to interpret, what is your "go-to" reaction? Do you respond immediately or take a moment to think? If you respond, do you typically strike with sarcasm? Or pepper them with accusations?

Journal a little about those thoughts...we aren't trying to solve something right now...just taking a moment to explore.

_____

_____

_____

_____

_____

_____

_____

CHAPTER 7

Unwanted and Alone

"Bare heights of loneliness...a wilderness whose burning winds sweep over glowing sands, what are they to Him? Even there He can refresh us, even there He can renew us." Amy Carmichael

Have you ever heard someone say, "I wouldn't darken the doors of that place"? According to Merriam Webster it means "to go to or appear at a place where one is not welcome anymore." Recently an article came out in a local magazine, a courageous woman shared her abortion story. Years ago, while attending a church, part of their music ministry, regularly singing from the stage, she had an abortion. Through her pain she shared her story with her pastor's wife. After praying with her, the time came for discussion about staying on the worship team. They asked her to step down. Her vow at the time was that she would never sing again.

When I walked into a church, I felt like I was wearing a blinking light. "Sinner!" "Bad woman here!" "Unworthy!" Overwhelming emotions would surface and I would cry buckets of tears. I decided at some point it was going to attract attention and someone would ask me too many questions. If they asked me too many questions and I told the truth, surely they would kick me out. Instead of taking that chance, I stopped going.

It's in the silence and the darkness,
those are the moments where whispers
of doubt and shame drown-out
every other voice, even God's.

In general, I have always been a very social person. Yet, I have been surrounded by people, laughing and talking, all the while inside I wanted to crawl into a corner. Feeling completely alone. Have you ever felt that way? Nothing feels more alone than having walked in confidence in a relationship with God, only to feel a million miles away from Him at some point.

When we feel separated from God, He didn't move, we did. I felt so unwanted by God because of my actions and the way I was living, surely He could never want or use me again. These were all lies from the enemy. Perhaps you've felt the same way? Let me assure you that the enemy's lies are always the same. Whether they come from your own thoughts, or someone else's words, anything that makes you feel unwanted and alone, is a lie.

When we internalize the lies, we begin to hate ourselves. Hating ourselves leads to our own mistreatment. Hating ourselves will affect every relationship in our life.

Ten years after my abortion I was married with four children, 2 step-sons and 2 I birthed. My nature seemed driven, and perhaps I was. Part of what kept me determined to push myself in all areas of life, was that it was a convenient way to keep my past from whispering in my ear. You know what I mean?

It's in the silence and the darkness, those are the moments where whispers of doubt and shame drown-out every other voice, even God's. I was on the path to destruction.

A friend of mine told me a story about her experience of leaving her husband of almost 20 years, for another man. Her current relationship was in shambles and she described "when I left my husband it was as if I took off running a sprint as far away from my current life as possible. Problem is, I ran a circle instead of a straight path, and as I rounded the circle I ran into a wall, smack-dab into myself."

Twenty years after my abortion, my life was right back where I started. A mess. My marriage was falling apart. My kids were hurting. My life was a lie! I was in the middle of hell on earth.

I had believed the lie whispered to me in the dark. In my mind, I created a God that turned His back on me because I was bad. Not that I had done something bad, but instead, I was bad, every part of me.

Instead of knowing what God says in His word repeatedly. He will never leave us or forsake us! Never means never! Deuteronomy 31:6 "...the Lord your God goes with you; he will never leave you nor forsake you." This is just one example where God promises to stay with us. God's Word is full of truth. Jesus was with me, even in the room when I had my abortion. I believe He carried my child, my daughter into Heaven. I believe she is there now, and one day I will be reunited with her.

Whatever the reason women choose to have an abortion, every woman has her own specific response and reaction. No one escapes. Even if you've lived a "normal" life since an abortion, without addressing what happened and seeking the Lord, there is a compensation made somewhere. I have yet to meet a woman who has not suffered in some way, usually silently, post abortion.

I mentioned a story about a woman who was asked to step down from her worship group after she shared about her abortion with her pastor's wife. Years later she mentioned to someone in a study group that she missed singing in church. A well meaning woman, trying to encourage her, made the comment that "God would use her again, and that she would sing again". This comment infuriated her. Why? Like picking a scab off a wound that has not completely healed, it bleeds again. Her scab had just been peeled off.

My wound had not healed. Pain and destruction left me broken. I realized it was time to make changes and face myself, and more importantly, face God. He already saw me, now I would turn around to see Him.

What was your thought when you read "Jesus was with me, even in the room when I had my abortion."? As a Christian - a follower of Jesus Christ, I believe His Holy Spirit lives in me. Even when I choose to make decisions for good or bad, I still have free choice. The term "my body, my choice" wasn't invented by the pro-abortion movement, God gave us free choice from the beginning of time. God gave us hints about which choice to make, several times throughout the Bible you will read where God offers life and death, blessings and cursings, and says…"choose life". Wow! How's that for love?

Have you had a moment when it felt as if the wound of pain was reopened? Write about that…what direction did you take after that…to seek more healing or to close off and hide?

_____

_____

_____

_____

_____

_____

_____

_____

_____

_____

_____

_____

_____

_____

_____

Where should you take the next step of healing? What does that look like for you today - a prayer - a song - a phone call - journaling?

_____

_____

_____

_____

_____

_____

_____

_____

_____

_____

Walking Into The Light

"The Christian life is not a constant high. I have my moments of deep discouragement. I have to go to God in prayer with tears in my eyes, and say, 'O God, forgive me,' or 'Help me.'" Billy Graham

It gives me comfort to understand that an amazing man, who walked as upright as any man since Jesus, Billy Graham, dealt with problems. In my life now, decades removed from the darkness I lived after my abortion, I understand clearly, we all will have trials and tribulations. No-one is immune. We have a tendency, however, to think when we see a person on television, or YouTube, or some sort of platform, what we see is who they are. Not always so. What we see in these various forms is a part of them. They have daily lives, with regular life issues just like us.

When we see the "humanness" of someone who seems to have it all together, it helps us to understand, our journey with God can bring us through any of these tough moments to rise above.

To walk in the fullness of all He created for us.

God's viewpoint on an unborn child is very clear. Did you know the Bible mentions unborn babies? In the story of Jacob and Esau we can read where God called the unborn babes. John the Baptist was unborn when he leapt in his mother's womb when Mary approached. God loved us before the foundation of the world! "Even before He made the world, God loved us and chose us in Christ to be holy and without fault in His eyes." Ephesians 1:4

Sparrows. Otherwise known as French Fry eating opportunists that hang out in the bushes at McDonald's. Well, that may not be an exact scientific definition. Out of curiosity I looked up some information about these seemingly "dime a dozen" birds.

There are 35 species of song sparrows alone in North America. Scientists say maybe up to 140 species of sparrows exist all over the world! In Bible days, when offerings and sacrifices were made, sparrows were used by the poor. Sparrows have never been on the endangered list and even in bible days, there seemed to be a surplus of the chubby looking birds. Yet, my precious friend, the Bible makes sure to give you one more way to grasp your value to our Father, God. Matthew 10:29-31 "Are not two sparrows sold for a penny? Yet not one of them will fall to the ground outside your Father's care. And even the very hairs of your head are all numbered. So don't be afraid; you are worth more than many sparrows." One translation says "more than a flock of sparrows".

When we see the "humanness" of someone who seems to have it all together, it helps us to understand, our journey with God can bring us through any of these tough moments to rise above.

God knew I would walk into the darkness that day so many years ago. He knew I would make every mistake I've ever made. Remember when I began this book I said "This is a love story"? God's overwhelming - love brought me out of the darkness and out of the deepest pit. Jesus showed me so lovingly and gently, that all my bad decisions then and now, show my need to walk closer to Him. Not that I won't ever fail, but in my failure, He brings victory to overcome. In my weakness, He is made strong. When I am upset and spent, He brings renewal. All of that began when I walked into a church with my husband, Tom Inman. I felt like every eye was on me in some way, or at best that if those people knew what I had done, that I had an abortion... they'd usher me out of that church and tell me to never return.

So where did I learn God's overwhelming love? I learned sitting in that church with my husband, that as the praise and worship would start, it was cleansing me. I would cry through the music, cry through the sermon, and my amazing husband had the grace to allow me to cry rivers of tears without ever asking me - why. He never asked me why I was crying, and for some of you, that may seem strange. I'm not saying he didn't want to know, I'm saying that he loved me so much, and he knew me so well that he knew if he had asked why I was crying, that I would have dried my tears and closed the door to my heart. And who knows where I would be today. That's where my healing journey began. And it was between me and God for quite a while. I will talk more about Tom Inman in another chapter.

A song written in the early 1900's reflects a beautiful sentiment of God's love for us through grace, through the blood of Jesus. Take a moment and meditate on this thought.

"Grace Greater Than All Our Sin"

(Written by Daniel B. Towner & Julia H. Johnston - public domain)

**Marvelous grace of our loving Lord,
Grace that exceeds our sin and our guilt,
Yonder on Calvary's mount outpoured,
There where the blood of the Lamb was spilt.
Grace, grace, God's grace,
Grace that will pardon and cleanse within,
Grace, grace, God's grace,
Grace that is greater than all our sin.**

Forgiveness and healing are different. Through Jesus, the blood He shed when He suffered and died, covered every sin you would ever commit. Don't get me wrong, it's not a "sin free" card. It is freedom of the highest imaginable form. When you come to Jesus and sinfulness is revealed, darkness actually flees and the glorious light of life and love of Jesus floods. We don't pretend everything is fixed at the moment of forgiveness, instead we walk into the freedom offered, and allow healing to begin. Healing is a process. Remember the scab we talked about earlier? Don't get frustrated with yourself, thinking you should be further along by now. If you find yourself repeating patterns of guilt, shame, anger, anxiety, depression or endless striving, you may still have unacknowledged pain unrevealed. Pray and ask God to show the inside of your heart, where the hidden places of your pain are, deep inside. Abortion isn't the only sin that causes these issues. If we aren't giving all of our sin to God, any of the missing pieces will not put the puzzle into place.

You may need another person to help you, Many times we do. There is no shame in taking time to seek professional help. I do recommend Christian counseling in order to blend the fullness of psychological and behavior training with the Word of God.

My story has mainly addressed those of us who have had an abortion. Or some of those who may have participated in allowing it to happen. Recently attention has been given again to those in the clinics performing the procedure. When we hear or read stories about men and women who have worked in those clinics, and then leave to follow Jesus Christ, stories are shocking. Many times we think of "those people" inside the clinics as inhuman or monsters. I am not going to begin a tirade about their reasons for working.

My reason for addressing this is to say, whatever side, receiving an abortion or performing the abortion, we pray. Simple as that.

We pray for all parties involved. We pray for our lawmakers as well. Prayer is powerful. Your voice is important. I believe God is calling the closet doors to open and allow voices of the silent to be heard.

My healing was not overnight. It took a long time. I continued to ask the Lord "show me" what I need to see for my healing. I wanted Him to show me the hidden places. Let us make our mission now, our prayer, "God, show me what's next. Take me to the next level." As we walk through our pain, into healing and wholeness, our love walk increases.

What is a "love walk"? You may have heard sermons where a person talked about the idea that our sin was put on Jesus when He chose to go to the cross. Jesus took our sin upon His body. As He was crucified, and dying, He cried out "Father, forgive them, for they don't know what they are doing". (Luke 23:34)

Love. As much as the truth of sin kept Jesus on the cross, it was love for us that caused Him to make the journey in Jerusalem, to be crucified, die and rise again. God loves us so much!

Tim Tebow was a college and NFL quarterback. During his college career in Florida he began putting bible references on the black patch under his eyes. His story is so beautiful. He put John 3:16 during the playoffs in college and 94 million people googled the scripture. This scripture reads, "God so loved the world that He gave His one and only Son, that whosoever believes in Him shall not perish but have eternal life." God - so - loved.

We pray for all parties involved. We pray for our lawmakers as well. Prayer is powerful. Your voice is important. I believe God is calling the closet doors to open and allow voices of the silent to be heard.

God loved us so much He gave. Now, we have the Spirit inside of us, we can love, we can give. We can love those who walk into an abortion clinic. We can love those who work in an abortion clinic. We can love those who pay for an abortion. We can love those who don't seem to love us. God's Spirit inside of us allows us to love the world. And that, my friend, is a love walk.

CHAPTER 8 JOURNAL

How do you deal with the daily walk of tuning out the voices that tell you God's grace isn't for you, that you've been too bad, gone too far? Do you have a regular routine that helps you continue to peel back the layers of your emotions in dealing with the abortion? Are you struggling with some of the fragments of anxiety, depression, shame, over-achievement, or anger? What has kept you stuck?

Maybe you aren't stuck. If not, do you find that although the memories won't ever be erased, your reaction time is farther apart? Are you bringing your memories to Jesus?

What about your love walk? How do you love those who were involved in your abortion? How do you love those who seem to be unlovable?

Journal about these thoughts today. Take a moment to allow God to reveal what the next step is for your healing. Do you understand the idea of grace? If you don't, look up some scriptures to keep close in your journal, reminding you it's not about working...it's about releasing.

_____

_____

_____

Loved

L-O-V-E-D

"We love others best when we love God most. The way we treat people we disagree with the most is a report card on what we've learned about love." Bob Goff

The love of God never changes. He never changes. God was God when I was innocent and pure. He knew when I would make mistakes and He loved me enough to allow me to make them. God also loved me enough to let me know the truth. My lies were not hidden. My sin was not in the dark. Not to God. "If I say, "Surely the darkness shall cover me, and the light about me be night," even the darkness is not dark to you; the night is bright as the day, for darkness is as light with you. For you formed my inward parts; you knitted me together in my mother's womb. I praise you, for

I am fearfully and wonderfully made. Wonderful are your works; my soul knows it very well....Search me, O God, and know my heart! Try me and know my thoughts! And see if there be any grievous way in me, and lead me in the way everlasting!" (Psalm 139:11-14 & 139:23-24)

Why was it so difficult for me to grasp the truth, that God never stopped loving me?

I mentioned earlier in the book that I grew up going to church. For me, church also represented the reminder that I had to "be good" in order for God to love me. Don't get me wrong, this isn't necessarily what was preached, it was however, insinuated. Some of you reading this experienced the same. A life of never feeling good enough for God is exhausting. Ultimately you may end up not even trying.

Why was it so difficult for me to grasp the truth, that God never stopped loving me?

In Psalm 103:12 we are reminded that "as far as the east is from the west, so far has He removed our transgressions from us."

Scientifically there is a north pole and a south pole. If you begin traveling from the north, you will reach the south. There is no east or west pole, or point where they switch, either magnetically or directionally. Such a path is simply circular - no beginning and no end.

Forgiveness with God, has no end.

My journey was and is, day by day. Understanding what God said about me was beginning to change how I saw myself. Change would not happen overnight. I found that learning what love was, would take time for me.

God introduced a man into my life several years after my divorce. I say God introduced us because Tom Inman would pray every night at his bedtime, "God, please send me a woman to love. You know I have a lot of love to give." Tom had been single for almost 10 years. Be careful what you pray! Although I chuckle at that statement, for Tom Inman, I was his answer. God would answer his prayer by bringing me into his life to give all the love to a broken woman, who needed to understand pure love from a man. Tom was the answer to a prayer I never knew how to pray.

My second marriage has taught me more about what God ordained for the "oneness" of a husband and wife, than I ever thought possible. Not perfection. Submitted to God and to each other, we have walked hand in hand through the healing of many wounds in our souls. Some we knew we had, some revealed as the years have passed. My husband is my rock. When I shared my story of my abortion with Tom, he simply loved me. No questions. No accusations. No further. He has never mentioned it unless I brought it up in conversation. When tears drenched my face during phases of healing, he would take my hand, no words needed. I love that man.

I realize not everyone has a Tom Inman, or trusted friend to share your story. Pray before you decide to share. You may need to seek professional counseling. I recommend a professional Christian counselor. When you open your heart to someone, you want direction to sound techniques, with Christian principles. Pray first. I pray for you to find just the right match if this is the route you choose.

Along the way, Tom and I began going to church regularly. Praying regularly. I began to read my bible every day. It took time. Time to sort through my beliefs from my previous teaching compared to what God says in the Bible.

My business employs a handful of people and they wanted to join me when I mentioned what I was doing. My mom lives outside of Oklahoma and a couple of others also wanted to read and discuss. They had begun to see major changes in me. Technology made it possible for us to join our office and others together on weekdays and discuss what we were reading in the Bible each day, live in the mornings. Following a daily Bible reading plan made it easy. We chose the translation we preferred and began. Now, years later, 5000 on my Facebook page, our daily Bible study with Elizabeth Inman is seen around the world! Overwhelming is an understatement!

My reason for sharing about this? My heart is for you to experience all God has for you. Individually. If you are sitting with my book in your hand, you are hungry for more. I know exactly what that feels like. I know the desire to connect to God, and be scared of God at the same time! Here's the beautiful, glorious news...God does have a "favorites" list. Guess what? You are on it! I am on it! All of humanity, before the foundation of the earth was added to the list. Not everyone will accept their role, but you will. You have a desire to know Him more. You picked up this book to read and are still reading because you long for depth with God.

Technology makes it easy to find Bible reading plans. Most will have an Old Testament, New Testament, Psalm and Proverb daily.

They have the date, without the year. By the end of the year, you have read the entire Bible! This breaks up into smaller portions which seems so overwhelming to most of us. When you begin, you may feel lost if you've never read before. In the Old Testament you'll get to lists of names - did you know there was an "Amaziah" and "Dodo" mentioned in the Bible? Neither did I until I read. As you read, pray. Pray for God to show you what you need for that day. If you've ever heard the story about Manna in the Bible, it was food each day, by God to the Israelites in the desert. It was only good for that particular day. Each day the Israelites needed a fresh batch. So it is for us with God's Word. Each day we pray and read, and reflect on how it applies to us. I've been doing this for a number of years now. It wasn't always like a bell rang and symbols crashed with a "word"! Sometimes it seemed like a whisper and I would wonder if I was doing this the right way. I never gave up! Don't give up! Keep going and you'll find day by day a change and so will those around you.

My 7–I'll go into more detail on these in Chapter 12. These are parts of my life that I make a priority and they have brought me through the process of healing out of the shame and misery I dealt with for so long. I began to make these 7 something that I incorporate in my ministry and through the years "My 7" are what I live by. Don't overthink them. Consider how to make the 7 a part of your daily living. When you do, you'll see changes in your life that you could have only imagined!

1. *Pray*
2. *Listen*
3. *Read*
4. *Gratitude*
5. *Give*
6. *Serve*
7. *Fellowship - Go To Church*

CHAPTER 9 JOURNAL

Have you struggled the way I did, accepting that God loved me? I remember it wasn't just about my abortion that I struggled, it was my contrary thoughts toward life. Life held no real value. I was going through the motions with my family and career. As everything seemed to begin to flourish on the outside my heart was breaking inside.

I mentioned one huge change for me was to go to church. Have you struggled going to church? What goes through your mind when you are sitting through the worship and message?

Have you struggled with understanding the depth of God's love for you? What is one step you can take today? Can you pray? Remember prayer, simply put, is talking to God. No "thee or thou" is necessary. He loves the sound of your voice. He created your voice.

Take some time to reflect on these thoughts today. And in case you haven't been told today...I love you and God loves you.

Courage my friend...take some deep breaths...pray, reflect, and write.

CHAPTER 10

He > I
(He is greater than I)

"We ourselves feel that what we are doing is just a drop in the ocean. But the ocean would be less because of that missing drop." Mother Teresa

About the time this chapter was written, I read another woman's story. Let's call her Ann. Ann shared on social media that she had two abortions. She wrote about her shame and torment, and self-loathing. Ann tried to have children later and miscarried multiple times. For her, this was punishment from God. Can anyone identify with that thought? Let me make clear. God does not take or maim a baby as "payback". God loves you and me, and most importantly, God - is - love. He does not punish, He frees. He does not wreck, He restores.

Consequences are not the same as punishment. In the Bible we read about this. "Do not be deceived, God is not mocked [He will not allow Himself to be ridiculed, nor treated with contempt nor allow His precepts to be scornfully set aside]; for whatever a man sows, this and this only is what he will reap. For the one who sows to his flesh [his sinful capacity, his worldliness, his disgraceful impulses] will reap from the flesh ruin and destruction, but the one who sows to the Spirit will from the Spirit reap eternal life." Galatians 6:7-8 AMP Through the years of all the Bible reading I've done, one thing is clear. When I ignore all the instructions for a good life, and choose to take my life into my own hands, without regard to God, it doesn't go well. Notice that scripture talks about reaping what a man sows? In the Old Testament it says (paraphrased) "I'm putting 2 options here before you, death and life....oh and by the way, CHOOSE LIFE!" (Deuteronomy 30:19) It doesn't say live a perfect life.

God never expects perfection, and all the role models in the Bible prove it. Yet, God used them mightily. Remember that as long as we live a life centered on 'my own way' and being the boss of my own life without regard to God, we will have consequences from our own reaping, not punishment from God.

Maybe you were the father of an aborted baby. Grandparent, sibling, cousin, friend or facility employee, or physician. Whatever your role in aiding for the abortion. What have been your consequences?

Ann went on to say it took decades for her to learn God does not punish for our sin. She learned her hardest path would be to forgive herself.

Another woman, another baby, another story. This is why I write. When we walk into a path God designs for us out of the pain, sometimes the question surfaces, "will this make a difference?".

I'm reminded of the story told about an old man, who lived on the beach. As he took his evening walk along the sand he noticed the tide had gone out and left what seemed to be thousands of starfish stranded to die on the sand. He walked along gazing with a hint of sadness for the beautiful dying creatures, he spotted a young boy at a distance. Closer now, he saw the boy pick up a starfish. He hurled it into the water. He bent down and plucked up another one and with an energetic toss, it too, landed in the ocean. Dutifully the man decided to teach the young boy a life lesson. He told the boy to look around, as far as they could see there were starfish, likely thousands of them. The man said "You are just a small boy. What you are attempting is kind and I understand you're simply trying to help. But young man you can't save all of them. What difference can you possibly make?" And the young boy thoughtfully considered the old man's comments and question. Then, he bent over and picked up a starfish and hurled it into the water. Splash! Then he turned to the old man and said "it made a difference to that one".

You were created to be here on earth at this moment for a purpose. Your life makes a difference. God would have sent Jesus to die on the cross just for you.

You were created to be here on earth at this moment for a purpose. Your life makes a difference. God would have sent Jesus to die on the cross just for you.

In the Bible a story explains that very idea...in Luke 15:1-7 "By this time a lot of men and women of doubtful reputation were hanging around Jesus, listening intently. The Pharisees and religion scholars were not pleased, not at all pleased. They growled, "He takes in sinners and eats meals with them, treating them like old friends." Their grumbling triggered this story. "Suppose one of you had a hundred sheep and lost one. Wouldn't you leave the ninety-nine in the wilderness and go after the lost one until you found it? When found, you can be sure you would put it across your shoulders, rejoicing, and when you got home call in your friends and neighbors, saying, 'Celebrate with me! I've found my lost sheep!' Count on it - there's more joy in heaven over one sinner's rescued life than over ninety-nine good people in no need of rescue."

If YOU were the only one...Jesus would have left the 99

for YOU! You are the reason I wrote this book. One life, one future, one dream, one hope at a time.

As you have walked through my book you may feel the urge to share your story with someone. My encouragement to you, make sure you only share your story within a safe relationship and a safe person.

Who are safe people? First of all, pray and ask God if this is the time and the person. Then take into consideration some things to ask yourself about the person. These are common questions that Christian Counselors, Therapists, and Psychologists often talk about when a person wants to answer, ***"Is this a safe person and relationship?"***

- **Does this person draw me closer to God or separate me?**

- **Does this person draw me closer to others or separate me?**

- **Does this person continue to point me to God and the Bible for answers rather than want me to follow them?**

There are books and workbooks through Christian Bookstores or online that can help you with boundaries and knowing how to stay free from unsafe relationships.

Living in truth does not equal condemnation. When our relationships are built on truth and grace through the Holy Spirit, healing conversations are able to take place. If you aren't sure who such a person would be, I urge you to talk with a Christian counselor first and they can walk you through steps for discussion.

I'm offering a lifeline of hope today. I live in freedom. I

stand in front of men and women who bravely share their stories, and I walk away whole. No longer am I bound to my pain. Freedom is possible!

I mentioned my early relationship with my mom a few times. Today, my mom and I have a beautiful, loving, mother-daughter friendship. I respect my mom for every decision she made during those years. She was simply doing the best she could, to no fault of her own. She loved me and was trying to protect me.

When we understand the enemy tries to separate us, especially our families, and will use any form he can, we see through those past moments and allow healing to begin. My mom is on the board of my ministry and I trust her with my life. She is a safe person for me.

CHAPTER 10 JOURNAL

You are valuable and precious. How does reading those words make you feel? Do you agree with the thought in this chapter that your life can make a difference?

As you have read my story, have you changed any previous view about yourself or your abortion? What are you sensing for the next part of your healing journey?

Take some time to write your thoughts at this moment. In the rawness of your feelings right now, write. You will find, as your healing continues, your writing will change, and so will your desires. By writing now, you will gain understanding as you progress. You'll look back to this time and see transformation.

_____

_____

_____

_____

_____

_____

_____

Loved

_____

_____

_____

_____

_____

_____

_____

_____

_____

_____

_____

_____

_____

_____

_____

_____

_____

_____

_____

_____

_____

_____

Where Do We Go From Here?

"While events cannot be unwritten, they can be redeemed"
Craig Groeschel

Writing my story of my life, abortion would be a chapter instead of a book. I would venture to say that is likely how you feel. And can we say at this moment together, "Thank God for that". Abortion was meant to destroy more than my child's life, it was meant to destroy mine, and my entire family, for generations to come. The devil didn't count on me finding out that in spite of all the crazy decisions men and women made in the Bible, God took what was meant to destroy them, and turned it for good, so that lives would be saved and changed. All through history the devil has tried to end the life of God's children. And the Bible is very clear. Storms of life will happen. It is clear to remind us that when the bad things happen, God will turn it for good. A story in the Bible tells the story of Joseph. It's in Genesis 37-50 and what Joseph endured, not many would survive. Just about anything bad that could happen, did happen to him. At the end of it all, when all the people who did horrible things to him, his very own family, wondered why he would be so good to them. His answer was the well known scripture from Genesis 50:20 "you meant it for evil, but God used it for good so that many lives would be saved". And he was talking about the saving of entire nations of people because of how God turned the bad to good.

The good news is that in spite of your poor decisions, in spite of the pain and mistreatment of others, you and I can hold on to the understanding of God taking those pains and poor decisions and turning them into something beautiful.

Even if today is the first time for you to understand that, your life changes this very moment into the goodness that God holds for you. This very moment!

Growing into the person God meant you to be will take some time. Changes take time. It's not a bad thing, be patient. I want to share some tools with you that have been my lifeline to help me arrive at the place of the healthy, whole woman that I am today.

The good news is that in spite of your poor decisions, in spite of the pain and mistreatment of others, you and I can hold on to the understanding of God taking those pains and poor decisions and turning them into something beautiful.

Keep in mind, I was still a mess when I began using these tools. I didn't have a manual with steps on how to build my life. Use what you want for you, and add other tools to your box if they fit better. You can formulate your own list. This doesn't even have to be your order. I am sharing with you what has worked for me now, to put me in a position of abundant successful living for almost 20 years. Join me now to discover the power of 7 tools that changed my life.

CHAPTER 11 JOURNAL

What chapter would the story of your abortion, or your experience with abortion be numbered? Why would you place it there?

What the book of your life be titled? If others you know, your parents, your spouse, your closest friend, were to title your book, what they call it, why?

Have you seen good come out of your story? If you answered "no". Think of it like this, I don't mean that you might not still carry shame or something like that. I want you to look a little closer at yourself. Do you have more compassion for someone who has to make a tough decision? Maybe that's all you can say at the moment, even if there is one thing you can see, it's there.

Do some examining to see where you've hardened and where you've softened. Write about both.

If someone came to you today with their story, what would you say to them?

_____

_____

_____

_____

_____

_____

_____

_____

_____

Elizabeth's Toolbox

1. PRAY: I know this step sounds simple. It is. Prayer has no prerequisite, no formality required. You might be saying "Elizabeth, is this really a tool? This is so simple!" If it's all so simple, when was the last time you prayed? I can remember a time when I would go days without praying. Prayer is essential every day, in fact, multiple times a day. When the Bible mentions to "pray without ceasing" (I Thess. 5:16-18), I don't know about you, but that was super intimidating to me! How on earth do I pray all the time?! What I've learned about prayer is that I can have a consistent "God awareness or God consciousness" as some call it, that keeps my mind on God all throughout the day. We make thousands of decisions every single day. Most of the time, without an awareness of them, and certainly not including God in any of them. I challenge you today to bring your awareness to keep prayer in the forefront of your day to day life, in addition to your bedtime prayer or mealtime prayer. Even what may seem the smallest decision, bring God in. The more time you spend with someone, the better you know them.

Prayer...it's number one and will change your life.

2. LISTEN: We can get so caught up in praying and asking and talking to God, that we forget to listen to what He has to say. If you and I were having a conversation right now and I did all the talking, you would be ready to say "shhhhh!" so you could have a chance to respond and share. God speaks through many forms.

God is as personal as your fingerprint. Here's how I've experienced God speaking to me. Through His Word. The more I've read, and asked God to show me what He wants me to see, it happens daily now that I see something in scripture newly revealed.

God speaks through circumstances. A friend of mine came out of a dire circumstance after her husband had taken his life. He left a path of bad debts to some very bad people and she knew her life and the life of her son might be in danger. As she prayed and asked God for direction on where to go and what to do, she got quiet in order for Him to speak. He showed her within a couple of days, through circumstances she never thought possible, God provided a safe place to live and to recover from the trauma. God speaks through peace. When we've asked God to help us make a decision, many times there may not be an arrow pointing toward the answer, instead you think about your options and you feel a peace toward one vs the other... that's God speaking. God speaks through our thoughts. And I want to be really clear on this...God will NEVER go against His Word. When a thought comes and you wonder if it's from God, it will have peace surrounding it, and will line up with life and love. Any thought to steal, kill or destroy in any form, is never from God. God speaks through nature. God speaks through wise-counselors. I have counseled many women and men through my Christ-Centered Counseling services. There is absolutely no shame in going to counseling for help, in fact, sometimes it's exactly the way God will speak to you. Use the tool of listening actively as you read further.

3. READ: I love peacocks. Until you just read that sentence, you had no idea about that part of me. You're reading my book which includes part of my life story. If we ever have the opportunity to meet in person someday, you will talk with me from the perspective of one chapter of my life. On the other hand, if I write my entire life story up to this point and you read that, you'll carry on a conversation with me from a deeper knowledge of who I am. You'll catch on to what I like, such as peacocks, and what I dislike, when a neighbor's cat makes its way into my yard to mark my bushes as its territory - in turn stinking up the bush as I walk by. So now you've read and you know me better.

LOL. When you read God's Word, you'll understand His love toward you.

BIBLE:
B-<u>Basic</u> I-<u>Instructions</u> B-<u>Before</u> L-<u>Leaving</u> E-<u>Earth</u>

Take time daily to spend reading the Bible, so you'll understand what to pray and how to listen.

4. <u>GRATITUDE:</u> Gracias, Merci, Arigato, do-jeh, Grazie, Spaciba, Danke Sehr, and thank you. Various languages, all a form of thanks. One of the most powerful tools in your toolbox will be this tool. Although it's listed fourth on the list, for me, this tool has dramatically changed my life and continues to this day. I lay in a fetal position on the couch one day, my first marriage, and the abuse was over. When you've lived in an abusive relationship, your life morphs into survival mode and changes your response from what most would consider normal. Instead of being glad to be out of something that was draining the life out of me, I was curled up on the couch and felt like I would die. I watched the clock tick by and thought, "If I can make it 10 more minutes, I'll be okay"....Ten minutes would pass...and I would repeat that cycle for a couple of days. Until finally, I got up and began to write.

My aunt sent a journal to me with the instruction to write 3 things I was grateful for each day. Keep in mind, I was still a mess. A mess! I thought God was still mad at me for my abortion. I began writing "Thank you for air"..."Thank you for my job"..."Thank you for my kids"... and as my thoughts continued, I was able to think of things gradually to add to the list. Gratitude reveals itself, the more you focus on it, the more you'll see opportunity to practice it. If you feel like you've been stuck in a place of any kind and can't seem to move forward, I encourage you to find a notebook, yellow pad, journal, of your choosing and write 3 things you're grateful for today. When you first get up in the morning, and again when you go to bed, begin and end your day with thoughts of gratitude.

How do you train to become an accomplished piano player? Practice! Every. Single. Day. How do you train yourself to be a person who lives in a state of gratitude? Practice! Every. Single. Day.

I have my degree in Psychology. It's fascinating to learn how our brain works in the areas of PTSD (Post Traumatic Stress Disorder) and something I've learned in my research, studying professionals in this area is that PTSD keeps people stuck in the past. Triggers of trauma bring a person right back to the moment in the past when the trauma took place and they relive it. God's desire and plan for us is to move into the present with a hope for the future. The most effective method I have found to achieve this type of thinking is "GRATITUDE". All of my teaching and training in counseling has helped me to realize "Gratitude" as a tool to keep a mind focused on the present, not past.

Psychologists have studied through the years to find that a practice of gratitude helps people sleep better, helps mental and physical well-being, and allows for better work function. Even if you only knew it would do that for you, isn't that a tool worth investing in? Use your gratitude tool today!

5. GIVE: God wants to be involved in your finances just like he does every other area of your life. The word of God has more to say about finances than it does about Heaven or Hell. Throughout the Bible we read that God has a lot to say about silver, gold, land, crops, animals, barns being filled, storehouses, wine presses, and we read about the wealthy and the poor of those days. Giving is never about what you're doing for someone else or something else, it is always, always about what giving will do for you. Where and to whom you give, is between you and God. My husband and I have given vehicles, furniture, clothes, lots and lots of money, and we have regularly given through our home, a place for people to live. This tool will change your life.

6. SERVE: For some of you this may be a no brainer. Some of you work in a profession where you serve every single day. The list would be too numerous to include everyone but some that come to mind are police-officer, sheriff, fire-fighter, nurse, physician, EMT, all of our armed forces, military, and so many others. Who makes the best leaders? The ones who are the best at serving.

There is a popular phrase that has come onto the leadership landscape called "Servant Leadership". It's not really a new concept, it has been a coined phrase since the 70's. But as far as current culture, it has become a tool that many companies embrace. Instead of the team rallying around the leader to prop him/her up, the leader rallies around his/her team to make sure their needs are met first. We can see this concept as far back as scripture. In Matthew chapter 20, we read the conversation Jesus had with some of his friends (disciples). A well-meaning mother came to Jesus to try and secure her two son's place at Jesus' side in the kingdom. As the conversation continued, the other disciples who were there were upset that the brothers might have a better place than they. Then Jesus turned the tables by saying "whoever would be great among you must be your servant". (verse 26) We see many times in the bible how those who became the greatest leaders began in some of the lowliest positions.

7. GO TO CHURCH: Our world has faced a changed landscape to some degree on what "going to church" might look like. When our world shut down to some degree, going to church wasn't an option. As I write this, here is how I suggest using this tool. Make intentional steps to be a part of a corporate worship group in some form, whether it's on a video platform, from your vehicle or maybe it's a small group of less than 10 people. My reason for encouraging you to be a part of a church body stems from how important it is for you to stay connected with other people. I cannot emphasize enough, isolation will never be a tool in my toolbox.

There is a difference between needing to have some quiet time, recharging your batteries alone. I am speaking of isolation where you don't gather with other believers in any form. When I thought God was mad at me, I absolutely was not about to go to church, where mistakenly I thought God only lived. Not going to church turned into not praying, not listening, not reading, no gratitude, no giving, no serving and then the cycle repeated...until next thing I knew, I was curled up on the couch counting minutes on a clock trying to survive one more minute.

Make the decision today to be a part of a church near you, if it's possible. If it's not, then join one online. Pray about where you should attend and listen, God will lead you!

CHAPTER 11 JOURNAL

Now it's time to create your own toolbox. What are the tools you plan to include? And why?

_____

_____

_____

_____

_____

_____

Are there any tools Elizabeth mentioned that you've never used before? Will you be adding them now? If yes or no, why?

_____

_____

_____

_____

_____

_____

_____

Which of all the tools is most important to you? Put the tools in order for you, and write a short note about why you have them in that particular order.

_____

_____

_____

_____

_____

_____

_____

_____

_____

_____

_____

_____

The Reason I Write

You. **The reason I write is you.** My story is not about me. I began by saying this is the story of God's unconditional love for me. Well guess what my dear, He is no respecter of persons. You are the apple of God's eye! You are on His mind right now, and right now, and right now, and yes, right now! Always! If you're thinking that you haven't felt very close to God for quite some time, He's not the one who moved.

I decided to lay down my life in this story for you my friend. This book is not just words on paper. It is my life. My real life. All the stories we read that are true stories, whether in the Bible or someone's life story, happened without a book being in the minds of any of those people. Men and women who are mentioned in the Bible didn't respond or think about their dialogue with the thought that someday, you and I would read about them. It may sound funny in a way, but sometimes we forget. This is real life... you and I are right in the middle of it right now. This isn't a dress rehearsal.

If you did the journaling, revisit the pages in a couple of months. Reading this book has opened windows of your soul to allow light to invade any dark places you've kept locked away. Now you will continue to be led into more and more freedom in Christ. Don't be frustrated with the pace. Allow the Holy Spirit to set the pace. He has a perfect plan. Our lives reach crossroads at various times. You are at one right now. As you set this book down, you will need to decide what is next.

PRAYER FOR YOU FROM ELIZABETH…

"Father God, I thank you for the person reading this.

Thank you for knowing every single detail of their life, even the things they keep hidden.

With you, God, there are no coincidences so I know it is on purpose they are reading this prayer and through it, they are receiving a major touch on their heart and on their life.

I thank you for blessing them and giving them a sense of connection with you right now they have never felt before. Thank you for the feeling of peace surrounding them that can only come from God.

Most of all, I thank you for giving them a sense of hope for their future; a hope that things will not stay the way they have been and the things to come are the best its ever been.

Father, thank you for showing us no wrong decision, no sin is too great for your love and your mercy.

Thank you for providing a path to healing and restoration for this person through you Son, Jesus.

Thank you for guiding them and for leading them and for always loving them.

In Christ I pray, Amen.

SCRIPTURES

2 Corinthians 1:4 Father of all mercy! God of all healing counsel! He comes alongside us when we go through hard times, and before you know it, he brings us alongside someone else who is going through hard times so that we can be there for that person just as God was there for us. (MSG)

Psalm 40:13 Be pleased, O Lord, to deliver me: O Lord, make haste to help me. (KJV)

I John 4:13-18 This is how we know we're living steadily and deeply in him, and he in us: He's given us life from his life, from his very own Spirit. Also, we've seen for ourselves and continue to state openly that the Father sent his Son as Savior of the world. Everyone who confesses that Jesus is God's Son participates continuously in an intimate relationship with God. We know it so well, we've embraced it heart and soul, this love that comes from God.

God is love. When we take up permanent residence in a life of love, we live in God and God lives in us. This way, love has the run of the house, becomes at home and mature in us, so that we're free of worry on Judgment Day—our standing in the world is identical with Christ's. There is no room in love for fear. Well-formed love banishes fear. Since fear is crippling, a fearful life—fear of death, fear of judgment—is one not yet fully formed in love. (MSG)

Hebrews 13:8 Jesus Christ the same yesterday, and to day, and forever. (KJV)

Jeremiah 1:5 Before I shaped you in the womb, I knew all about you. Before you saw the light of day, I had holy plans for you. (MSG)

Revelation 21:4 And God shall wipe away all tears from their eyes; and there shall be no more death, neither sorrow, nor crying, neither shall there be any more pain: for the former things are passed away. (KJV)

Matthew 18:21-22 At that point Peter got up the nerve to ask, "Master, how many times do I forgive a brother or sister who hurts me? Seven?" Jesus replied, "Seven! Hardly. Try seventy times seven. (MSG)

Jeremiah 29:11 For I know the plans I have for you," declares the Lord, "plans to prosper you and not to harm you, plans to give you hope and a future. (NIV)

Romans 8:28 And we know that all things work together for good to them that love God, to them who are the called according to his purpose. (KJV)

Psalm 102:18 This shall be written for the generation

to come: and the people which shall be created shall praise the Lord. (KJV)

Isaiah 6:6-8 Then one of the seraphim flew to me with a live coal in his hand, which he had taken with tongs from the altar. With it he touched my mouth and said, "See, this has touched your lips; your guilt is taken away and your sin atoned for." Then I heard the voice of the Lord saying, "Whom shall I send? And who will go for us?" And I said, "Here am I. Send me!" (NIV)

Exodus 14:13 Do not be afraid. Stand firm and you will see the deliverance the Lord will bring you today. (NIV)

Psalm 27:13 I will remain confident of this: I will see the goodness of the Lord in the land of the living. (NIV)

I John 4:4 You, dear children, are from God and have overcome them, because the one who is in you is greater than the one who is in the world. (NIV)

I John 4:7-10 My beloved friends, let us continue to love each other since love comes from God. Everyone who loves is born of God and experiences a relationship with God. The person who refuses to love doesn't know the first thing about God, because God is love—so you can't know him if you don't love. This is how God showed his love for us: God sent his only Son into the world so we might live through him. This is the kind of love we are talking about—not that we once upon a time loved God, but that he loved us and sent his Son as a sacrifice to clear away our sins and the damage they've done to our relationship with God. (MSG)

Made in the USA
Columbia, SC
17 June 2021